THOUSAND STAR HOTEL

Also by Bao Phi

Sông I Sing

THOUSAND STAR HOTEL

Bao Phi

COFFEE HOUSE PRESS

Minneapolis

2017

Coffee House Press books are available to the trade through our pri-
mary distributor, Consortium Book Sales & Distribution, cbsd.com or
(800) 283-3572. For personal orders, catalogs, or other information,
write to info@coffeehousepress.org.

Coffee House Press is a nonprofit literary publishing house. Support from
private foundations, corporate giving programs, government programs,
and generous individuals helps make the publication of our books possible.
We gratefully acknowledge their support in detail in the back of this book.

LIBRARY OF CONGRESS CATALOGING-IN-PUBLICATION DATA

Names: Phi, Bao, 1975– author.
Title: Thousand star hotel / Bao Phi.
Description: Minneapolis : Coffee House Press, 2017.
Identifiers: LCCN 2016051821 | ISBN 9781566894708 (paperback)
Subjects: | BISAC: POETRY / American / Asian American. |
    POETRY / Asian.
Classification: LCC PS3566.H467 A6 2017 | DDC 811/.54—dc23
LC record available at https://lccn.loc.gov/2016051821

PRINTED IN THE UNITED STATES OF AMERICA

24 23 22 21 20 19 18 17   4 5 6 7 8 9 10 11

Contents

1   Say WHAT?

I.

5   Vocabulary

7   Cookies

8   Shell

9   Go to Where the Love Is

11   Lead

14   The Reveal

16   Kids

19   Want to Want

21   When My Daughter Asks Me to Check and Make Sure Racists Can't Come In and Kill Us

22   Our Minnesota

25   Peeking through the Back Door of the Commodore

27   Refugees from the Prom Center, the Eighties

28   The Why

29   To Combust

31   Knockoff

34   The Measure

36   Poem for Ahmed Al-Jumaili

38   List of Notable Asian American Poets

39   467 / 500

40   Frank's Nursery and Crafts

41   "Allies" Who Think They're the Chosen Ones

42   Are People of Color as Bad or Who's Bad or Bad Meaning Good

43   Bad Driver, or Asian American Activists Who Talk about Their Own People Like They Are "Other"

45   It Was Flame

46   Oriental Flavor

47   Token Exceptional Asian in Liberal Multiculturalism

48   At Dinner

50   April 30, 2014

52   Apple-Red Pathfinder

54   No Question

56   Villain/elle: Shimomura Cross Over in the Flat of the Night

57   Rolling through a Four-Way

58   Bầu Cua Cá Cọp

II.

61   Future Letter to Daughter Apologizing for When I Caved to Her Request and Brought Her to Barbie's Dreamhouse at Mall of America

62   Broken Things

65   Document

68   Lights

69   In the Dark

70   Careful What You Wish For

71   Tourist with Daughter

72   Contour

74   Full Contact

75   Geek Triptych

77   Balsa Wood Free Association

78   For All Heartbroken Pizza Delivery Boys

80   Theresa, I Think

81   Incomplete / Abridged

86   Therapist 4

88   Chess Pride, Waverly Style

89   Night of the Living

93   Mouse

94   For Brandon Lacy Campos

95   Well Then

96   In Harbor

III.

101   Ego-Tripping as Self-Defense Mechanism for Refugee Kids Who Got Their Names Clowned On

102   Not a Silverfish

104   Being Asian in America

105   Untitled / Fathers

106   Thousand Star Hotel

107   Refugerequiem

109   Acknowledgments

THOUSAND
STAR HOTEL

Say WHAT?

—The word "ma" means six different things in Vietnamese,
depending on the tone

Ma—ghost—even with no tone to fetter, it lives
Mà—but—say this like you're laying it down
Mả—tomb or grave—curl it like a question mark
Mã—horse—start from the bottom, then go up, like ghetto dreams
Má—momma—the one I didn't have to look up
Mạ—to plate—heavy, a stone too large for your hands, dropped in water

Vietnamese people have always been spoken word poets.
How you say it
is as important to the life of the word
as the word itself.

I.

Vocabulary

—With thanks to Guante

Maintenance, they called it.
Minimum wage to guide shopping carts
from parking lot to corral.
We lined those silver metal buggies
with red plastic-flap seats for infants
into rows of ten to twelve,
up to thirty if you were a team of two.
Keep at the push long enough,
those stacked trains would roll—
the hardest part was steering.

One winter, a fellow cart pusher confided in me during a lull
as we stood near the weak warmth of the rattling heat vent in the cart corral.
Like me, he was a nonwhite boy from a poor family.
Like me, his face was limestone and granite pressed tight together.
His eyes distant, he spoke of how much he missed his girlfriend,
how they had been reunited the night before.
Yesterday night, we got back together, and I fucked the shit out of her,
I missed her so much.
He said it like their love
saturated every atom of his being
and shook him,
as if all his veins were laid bare
to weep at the memory of her,
as if his ache for her was a chasm
he could never hope to cross,
only tumble into headlong.
Timid virgin that I was,
my eyes wide open as if he had just tried to convince me
of a God I didn't think could exist,
I nodded sympathetically.
Sobbing, he wiped his eyes
stormed away from me

into the slush,
ashamed
of laying his emotions so bare,
and never talked to me about her again.

Now, over twenty years later
I make my living with words.
But all I can say about the bombs that sought my family
is: they missed us.
I still can't reach out to my friends,
especially my fellow straight boys,
their eyes the size of stop signs.
I find myself wanting to tell my mother and father I love them and
I just
can't.

I think about that boy,
in that cold cart corral,
how he found
the only words he could—
perhaps more importantly—
the vocabulary to overcome himself.

And I wonder
if I ever will find a language
to speak of the things
that haunt me the most.

Cookies

For the holidays, our Lutheran sponsors used to give us a blue cookie tin. Within lay two layers of small hard cookies separated by little white paper cups with frilly edges. My five siblings and I, we'd fight over the round ones with sugar sprinkles. For Christmas my sister gave my daughter a box of shortbread cookies shaped like Scottish terriers. She wanted to share them with me, and they tasted so much like those cookies from our childhood I had to close my eyes and look away. Her five-year-old eyes track some commercial in which white men are playing at battle and she asks me about war. I want to tell her that her grandpa once told me how one of his friends on the front lines got hit in the side with a rocket while crawling out of a foxhole, and he had to pick up smoking pieces of him and put him into a cookie tin to send the remains to his family. I want to say that one of the few things my father showed me from Vietnam was a black-and-white photo of him and his brother; one day I will have to find a way to tell her how he was killed. Or my father will tell her, if he can bear to tell it in English. I want to say *I am made of war and that means so are you.* I want to say *I was born inside a halo of gunpowder. No—a silhouette of a circle left by an exploding bomb. No—a snake eating itself.* But instead I take a deep breath and begin to tell her, *Your Ông nội, he fought in a war, along with many others, and like many others he didn't want to. And that's why I am here and you are here. And that is why sometimes other people look at us and they don't know why we are here and sometimes that makes us feel like we don't know, either.* And like so many other times, I don't know how to end these truest of stories. At the end I say nothing; I just look into her eyes, wishing I could say *surviving all of this makes you tough.*

Shell

Brown people getting bombed—
how can you
even think
about

love?

But you do.

You don't want to be
thankful it's not you—
you want to
wrap your arms around all of it.

You can't.

The news crackles
     drones drop
     blossoms
     empty
     the heads of children
     no science fiction
     to save them.

You'd settle for a tattoo of a heart
an empty outline
an approximation
of a thing.

You can't control the beating.

Go to Where the Love Is

Now there is a high fence
around mom's garden and the sidewalk.
Wood and chain link.
Thunderdome of the ghetto.
A dope boy had run in,
ditched something,
police with their dogs spent two days
turning it all over,
dirt to ditch
in search of proof—
these things that have nothing to do with her.

More than two decades ago she was squatting,
fixing up damage
someone had inflicted on the easiest of targets:
the gooks in the hood.
Across the alley,
a multiculti rainbow of boys
shouted insults at her,
Asian and *Woman*
forged in translation into slurs
cutting and rusted,
tearing and worn,
needing no translator in order to wound,
they were endlessly full of youthful breath:
a hurricane never grows tired.
It destroys until it doesn't.

She won't call the police:
Vietnamese people know
people in uniforms
make things worse.
I stood there and could say nothing.
Not even that I'd write a poem about it twenty years later.

The worst powerlessness
is when wicked men and boys
come for your family
and you can do nothing.

Now behind her high fence
she gives cucumbers to my daughter,
asks me to fix her Vietnamese cable channels.
I don't know how.
She says she'll die in Vietnam.
She has always said this.

It is quiet all around.
She opens the heavy gate,
nothing on the other side
kept out.
Stretching both ways the sidewalk is gray and smooth,
perfect even where it is cracked.

She smiles,
does not even look
beyond the fence.
I don't ask
if she remembers.

She sends me home
with bags of food
she made herself.

Love is not neutral.

Never.

Lead

Dad squats under the sun
patching with trowel and wet cement,
gray swaths in the shapes of leaping dolphin backs
before being blurred into the chink.
This is not the first time he has had to fix
vandalism against us,
the ones in the hood who everyone can agree
are to blame for some war that left everyone here
smoking and threadbare.

I'd rather be at the Franklin Library, learning the difference
between basilisk and cockatrice,
Theseus and Perseus,
heroes with names we want to pronounce.

Dad complains about mosquitoes.
He swats.
I wish I were somewhere else.
I fancy myself Luke Skywalker of the hood,
in lieu of white skin and blue eyes,
a towel for a cape and a flashlight,
instruments that make me a good guy.

He jerks in the heat,
curses in Vietnamese,
hollers for me to look around
for a shooter
            like it's the DMZ
claims someone is shooting a BB gun at his back.

I am ashamed. Why does my dad
see the enemy hiding

everywhere.

Why does he insist the Communist bullets have found him
here,
finally,
in Phillips,
home of the AIM patrol
and a park called Cockroach
kids clowning each other
for accepting free cheese
when we know
all our families do.

I want my dad to be normal
not yell in his foreign tongue
that everyone is out to get him.
I am sure they're just mosquitoes
but I am too scared of him
to tell him.

I am sure they are just mosquitoes
even when I see dull lead fragments sticking
into his brown skin.
I didn't want to believe him,
even as I helped him wash his wounds.

You need someone to care for your life,
or at least your dignity.
My dad had a son who believed in invisible mosquitoes
more than the evil of men.

Darth Vader had a son who could not understand
his father had been corrupted into killing the best version
of himself.

My dad had a son who thought he was just another gook who didn't know what caused him pain.

They say we're all equal, but we are the ones standing here with the history of our fathers' blood on our hands.

The Reveal

On a slow night, two Chinese boys in hoodies
kick a hacky sack under the lights
in the parking lot outside their family's restaurant,
the asphalt a black and blacker ocean
stretching past neon signs now turned off
save for the promise of an all-you-can-eat buffet.

Haloed in light, they could be anything:
overworked, bullied, heartsick, in love.
What can you do but guess?
Asking would ruin their moment.
They are not about you anyway—
what passes between them is in slow arcs
ignoring thick, painted lines beneath them
they will negotiate, enforce their own rules.

When you were a boy, this parking lot
was vast, littered by tall white buckets
and punctured Lysol cans.
That's how the homeless got high,
your friends told you.

> Inside, you wait for your mom to get off work.
> An elderly white man asks you questions as you shift
> from foot to foot,
> then offers you a dollar
> to come home with him.
> You say nothing,
> except no.

> Your mom's coworkers from the fabric store come out later.
> They wished you'd told them earlier, they say,
> hands on your shoulders,
> their eyes turning back and forth to scan

the brick horizon,
clutching at you like a boat almost lost to sea.
I'm okay, you want to say to them.
I'll be okay.

Years from that moment you step into a parking lot
and the flat land reveals the entire sky to you.
Immense, total, blue,
the cars and concrete
a tiny fraction lining the bottom
of your vision.
Condos now,
and a Chinese restaurant,
the night falling
and never righting itself
two boys playing hacky sack
stuffing their hands into their pockets,
laughing into the dark
as if they can't believe
what they are doing,
bored already,
heads tilted back,
faces eclipsed by the edges
of their hoods.

Kids

—I know there is a greater chance that someone will call my daughter
a chink than she has a chance of finding true love. —David Mura

In a dark back corner of me I didn't want to have kids.
How much blood and history can one last name hold.
Others in my family tell me what they did to survive to come here,
and who didn't.

You should be glad to be in America, it's better for your kind here
The opposite of history is erasure.

All of you are fresh off the boat and should be grateful we even let you in
Asian Americans are the opposite of history.

Go back to where you came from
Erasure is the opposite of survival.

A boy on the school bus says I have a flat face like someone smashed it
with a frying pan.

All the kids laughed at his poetry except him.

He stared at me, a monster from his comic book,
could not look away.
I was not a boy but a movie about demons,
his eyes bright bulbs of a projector,
my face a flat screen.

No one will see past the flatness of our faces.
They mistake those full horizons for blankness,
will mock our mouths without understanding our tongues,
chant
chink
gook

chink
gook
at my
family until my family retreats.
No one cares where.

My daughter is not yet five when she learns to be scared of racists,
yet smiles at every playground
even the one where a herd of kids
chanted
chink
chink
chink
in unison at her daddy when he was a little boy
a chorus to the only song one of us could ever belong to.

What promise is there except those chants,
words that grind cinders into skin never thick enough,
until she won't want to be herself at all—
will she be hated as
a gook first or
a woman first
or a dyke or
will there be new words
for her balled all into one,
hands digging into creased school bus seats to brace against
words that have nothing to do with her and are meant
only
for
her

What promise is there but flocks of bullies
flitting as they follow her home
fists dropping,
the opposite of feathers

Will anyone ever ask if the shadows in the corners
have ever been lit to wing
so that in dreams she can lift to love
without wondering if she deserves it

Can she crack a window and breathe a world
breathing her back—
a lung we are
but we keep tarring
smoking
these bellows
the life we deserve
but that our kids don't.

How much energy will I spend trying to defend her against men not at all
    like me

                                 and exactly like me
You can't protect her

she's not a map
she's a globe
she is not the playground
she is the falling and the getting up
teeter-totter of a daughter
she wears the easiest part of you to see
she wears the worst part of you
she wears your face

Want to Want

I want to *want to* wake up in the morning.
Instead I bookmark an ad for an alarm clock
with an arm attached to it—
slaps you in the face to wake you.

Before the sun rose and before he took the long bus to work
my dad shook my shoulder; we'd amble to fish
from some mucky pond by the side of a crumbling highway,
the fire he let me make on the shore
really just twigs of daddy longleg thickness and toilet paper,
very little light and even less warmth but all the danger.

Some days I would wake up and drive moon boots into
blue-white snow blushed with the last dark of night to catch a bus
to a windowless school.

Now everyone on the TV is telling me to run off and have adventures and
    move to another country and speak another language really badly
    while wearing cute jeans before it's too late, but it was too late a few
    too lates ago.

I didn't watch football until my daughter was born, and now it's too late
    to stop watching even though I know we'll always lose.

She has grown from sleeping against my stomach
to playing at my feet and declaring that her favorite team is my team, and
    she doesn't
know football but that she likes what I like anyway
and I want to put her in a time capsule forever—
even when her tantrums shake my teeth
from their sockets.

She is perfect, and the road of life to wherever the fuck
can be wherever the fuck and whatever the fuck

because she is perfect
right now,
even when she won't let me sleep,
her elbows digging into my back,
my face buried away
from the morning.

When My Daughter Asks Me to Check and Make Sure Racists Can't Come In and Kill Us

Everybody
argues / confesses
about privilege
until
the echo becomes a kind of din.

Conversation is good,
I suppose, but
that's not what this is.

Macbook Marxist.
Powerbook Colonialist.
iPhone Antiracist.
Pizza-Franchise Conservative.

Compare oppressions like dick sizes.

We argue on the internet while our kids beg us to lock the windows
    and doors.

Our Minnesota

Pass the pool hall where Viet men stood
in smoke, dim ghetto kings,
cash a green tide yoked under a gold clip.

Pass the gun shop next to the Chinese chicken wing joint,
the sneaker store that squeaked by for decades.

Pass the thrift store bakery where your father bought you
expired treats, the multiple homicides of crows
like a black snowstorm in bare Powderhorn branches.

Pass the dull concrete where the pay phone
once stood sentry, more tags than quarters, the boy
who always asked if you wanted to join the 'Lords.

Pass the intersection that held Viet and Latinx barbers
and Somali cell phone stores,
the burnt ghost of the Commodore bar.

Pass the chicken coops, the gentrification
that allows you to afford
pretty hardwood floors
if you put up with the stray bullets
passing right through the drywall.

Pass the forgotten paper route, rolled newspapers
thrown in the garbage, the European immigrant
who laughed when you caught her stealing her neighbor's coupons.

Pass your years at the shitty Tex-Mex restaurant
where the hot hip white people slept with one another
and scorning one another's music taste was a point of pride.

Pass the Little Earth projects, AIM patrols in red trucks
armed with baseball bats,
the park we learned to call Cockroach,
the kids who smiled when they asked if you wanted to play.

Pass the bullet hole missing the haunt of its smoke.

Pass the 21A and its late song.

Pass the broken glass, translucent shark fins cemented on top of backyard
    gates.

Pass the gas station horoscopes rolled tight as cigarettes.

Pass the thin brown carpet where you lay down and could not believe any
    further in true love.

Pass the brown women and men practicing their dances in the front yard.

Pass the parking lot where that boy flashed a gun.

Pass the asphalt where you did the worm and landed your first kickflip,
the hungover white Vietnam Vet and the Black Panther,
both of whom wanted to teach you karate to defend yourself.

Pass the empty lot your older brother convinced you was haunted,
even the flashlight you pretended was a lightsaber did not give you courage.

Pass the ghost of your first kiss on the playground at Anderson Elementary,
by beached concrete playground cylinders that looked like bomb shelters.

Pass the loops of graffiti, arches of bridges collapsing on themselves.

Pass the street whose number you don't even know,
a lover's curve starting between McDonald's and 35W
back to Phillips, by the beautiful office building that made weapons of war.

Pass a small brown boy in a Batman shirt,
pointing at you, teaching himself to say your name
not so far from where, years before,
kids found a way to make your alien name
a wound.

Pass every streetlight,
without your glasses they look so much like stars.

Peeking through the Back Door of the Commodore

—For R. Vincent Moniz Jr.

Glow and ping of pinball.
A fan blowing,
oil-slick rainbow arch of a jukebox.
Windowless dark is where adults do adult things.
Far from here and years later,
young white people will make bars with floor-to-ceiling glass
so all can see who they're drinking with,
brew their own beer and whisper recipes,
charcuterie techniques—
over which they will fall in love.
In Phillips the Commodore may or may not have been filled
with drinkers who definitely could not give a shit if you saw them.
Little brown boys who illegally skateboarded
in the shadows of buildings named after big men,
we walked by quiet—
as if God were watching as we knew she was—
rectangle of dark, open in the bright sun of a school day.
I could tell you there were noises of pool cues
struck on the side of scuffed tables,
jagged ends jabbed at friends drunkenly confessing
sleeping with so-and-so's wife,
cowboy music followed by 80s R & B
quips switchblade quick
about fuck your football team and so-and-so's music is bullshit and
it's all going to shit anyway, but
I'd be lying.
Mostly that square dark door stayed
dark and quiet.
Reading too much Greek mythology
did the rest.
Vince says, *I thought that place*
was so soaked in blood and tears
it would never burn down.

But by now we should have known
that even dark, quiet nothings
are quickly lit to flame.
Now there are just whispers
of adults with no corners to haunt,
nothing to mark a space
God kept her eye on—
not even a cinder.

Refugees from the Prom Center, the Eighties

Who says Asians can't dance?
Old Viet people can cha-cha and tango
like their feet and hips
asked to be colonized.

You can't handle them, so don't.

I'm walking with kids older and taller
blocks away, the promise of video games
in some arcade, or maybe the front of a store.

I hate Vietnamese people, one of the boys says suddenly,
scowl like a blue-marbled switchblade.
I hate my own people, he laughs,
to make sure we get it.

I've only got one quarter.
So I hold it in my palm
and watch the other kids play
including the hater,
who puts his quarter into a slot
does his best to control
his one man of three.

Can't remember what game he played,
or whether I cared that he hated Vietnamese people like me,
like him.

That's a lie.
I know I didn't care.
I was rooting for him,
even after I saw him lose
man after
man.

The Why

At a prison reading
the majority of the audience was from my neighborhood:
the guys shouted out *Phillips*
as if welcoming home one they once thought alien.
A beautiful black transwoman asks for my autograph.
I want to ask her story, but she walks out smiling
with the loops of my name on a page
while I stand there silent.

They've come to listen to the art that kept me out of this place
but I'm still the one that gets to walk through those detectors
to whatever I call home.

Now I want my daughter
to have some record of this man—
sashimi-thin when the world doesn't want to see me,
fatty pork when they need to hate me—
they'll consume me and there will be only silence.

A book can be another empty space
I could have been, a ghost haunting the margin—
no words to describe himself.

To Combust

When his oldest son comes home from the corner gas station
beaten for no reason
we can venture to guess Dad sees blood and thinks
how he risked his life to get us all on that plane,
jumping in, last minute,
prayer and opportunity,
looking over his shoulder once
to see shells dropping where we once stood
before becoming an alien to his homeland forever.

On to working at a sewing machine,
a bus stop where he fought off muggers a third his age.
Tried to raise six kids, we a Swiss Army knife
left open in his pocket, all sharp-edged and crazy in different ways
drawing blood when he reached in.

His wife,
but not for much longer,
yelling at him in the driveway,
in English,
in front of the nice Lutheran sponsors.

He mutters in his sleep;
in the dark we'd listen,
fists to our mouths to stifle our laughter
until we realized it was about war.

He looks out and sees how combustible everything is.
How we could all just become
flashes of flame, then nothing.
He doesn't ever want to be an American:
they say they will be there for you but won't.

Bruises and blood on his oldest.

Of course, nothing in life can
ever be good.

He gets a two-by-four.

Small curls in the wood's flesh
where the saw cut it.
Walks to the gas station,

sobbing.

He wants to know
who hurt his son.
He wants to kill someone,
the language he is always reminded

he understands.

Knockoff

—With thanks to Juliana Hu Pegues for the observation that Asians are always interrogated, and inauthentic, in America.

Fake Gucci fake Prada fake Burberry in a fake store
in a fake part of town shielded by a fake dragon façade
Fake weave made with real black-licorice hair
Fake housing projects
Fake mansion in Bel Air
Fake fingernails and real toxins in real lungs
Fake eyelids make flutters in fake mirror
paid for by real dollars
Fake high-wire kung fu fake hero fake man
Fake tech boom
Fake Silicon Valley
Fake red blush flush with success
Fake inflation fake gentrification
Fake love making
Fuck your little dick
wrong slant pussy
fake sex fucking
Fake soldier
see if you can fake this hazing
Fake struggle
real bullets
real deportation
Fake strength—oh you complaining with your fake weakness
Shut the fuck up fake activist
fake minority
fake white person
fake person of color
fake feminist
fake queer
fake working class
fake poor
fake oppression

Fake your thank-yous
you should be glad you're even here with your
fake gratitude
fake longitude
fake latitude
Fake-ass poet unless
you're a real white poet with a fake
Chinese name that belongs
to a real person in which case
let us taste your funk
but otherwise fuck your fake fusion
fake chink—no wait you're a gook
You fake slope
no
You fake dothead
no
You fake raghead
no
You fake flag on the front door threadbare
You fake and taking up space but can't see how much
through your slanted eyes
You fake Nike swoosh flailing in a factory
You fake iPhone 6, 7, 8 suicide
You fake NBA player overrated chink in a jockstrap
Fake boat but real leak
Fake pirate but real rape
Fake passport but real pat down
Fake concentration camp but real internment
Fake railroad but real bang
Fake English speaker on the other end of a tech help line
Fake scientist selling secrets to Japan
no wait China
no wait Korea
Fake ID
Fake English
Fake country

Fake fault line
Fake demarcation
Fake citizen
Fake American
Fake eyes
Fake face
Fake arms
Fake legs
Fake voice
Fake your
every
little
part

The Measure

—With thanks to Jon Schill

On June 23, 1982, Vincent Chin died from wounds sustained in an attack from two working-class white men who blamed him and the Japanese auto indus-try for the loss of their jobs, even though Chin was Chinese American and did not work in the auto industry. One man held him in a bear hug so the other could strike him four times in the head with a baseball bat. As his brain leaked onto the sidewalk, Chin's last words were reportedly, "It isn't fair." His wedding guests attended his funeral instead. The men who killed him, to this day, have not spent a day in jail nor paid any of the $3,700 fine. The judge presiding over the case said, "These aren't the kind of men you send to jail."

Listen carefully:
this is how
white people tell

     you

that "you can be anything you want as long as you work hard enough"
does not apply to

     you
or
   your
      children.

If you forget,
they will apply

pressure

on the sidewalk,
in front of

   witnesses.

                Lily and David Chin,
in laundries and restaurants and in a brush factory,
worked all their lives to see their

                son

murdered twice.
If ever
                I
am to stand in front of a judge
to measure the dollar amount of
                my
life
and he cannot decipher
what kind of man
                I

am
how
                I

will haunt history

                I

will tell him

                I

am what

                I

always have been:

                I
am a dead man.

Poem for Ahmed Al-Jumaili

The shower:
water looks like elongated beads of silver
each with a band of shifting rainbows at the top.
Those who shower before the sun comes out
only see this when they are late—
sunlight turning hyphens of water into the briefest art,
dying down the drain.

Twenty days ago it was ISIS and before that, them—
or rather, some form of us—
men, uniforms, twisting
tornadoes of smoke and fire
into the skies of Iraq.
You fled here, like my people did.
You took pictures of your first snowfall.
Usually seen only when enlarged for official Christian holidays,
made of construction paper,
the real thing falling now from the Texas sky:
frozen microscopic fingerprints.

No one knows why they shot you.
There are bullet holes.
There is blood.

There are myths about hundreds of words for snow,
if you lived your life
surrounded by it.

Why then are there not a hundred words for bullets,
for running into the aiming eyes we are taught are civilized,
meaning safety—
instead fleeing to this country made of
crosshairs.

I wish you a flurry of peace.
I wish you the slush avalanched forth from mourning.
I wish you justice, so thick
it covers this land all around us.

List of Notable Asian American Poets

On a clothesline: a constellation of lynched Chinamen.
Bleach,
then hang dry.

War
Deportation
Bombing
Chink
Refuge
Buddha:
for lexical repetition in a sestina.

Dudes who think they're more Asian than us
because they married one of us.

White teachers in the hood
who don't think Asians are oppressed enough
to need saving.

No sainthood without a headline.
No headline that needs a translator.

You don't survive by putting to paper
what happens behind the restaurant's doors to the kitchen.
The fortune is not the fortune, it's the cookie.
Those who can eat will eat.
All the while wolves in gatekeepers' clothing
check off boxes.
This is how we divide sheep.

467 / 500 (Asian Americans Are an Interrogation Waiting to Happen)

All Asian American fans will now be forced to show ID at basketball games to prove they are an authentic fan of basketball and not just jumping on a Jeremy Lin bandwagon. They will be required to pass a test with questions such as

1) what is a triangle offense?
2) what state does the city of Los Angeles reside in?
3) name five current NBA coaches (D'Antoni, McHale, and Woodson don't count)

Failure to present this ID will result in the fan being detained over by the nachos, where they will be forced to answer where they are from— no, where are you REALLY from—and why they like basketball. Asian American sportswriters will be required to write a 1,200-word personal narrative describing when they started to like basketball and why. If, within the essay, they mention they played basketball, they must specify whether it was in J-town leagues, Chinatown leagues, or against *real* players—and if the latter, they must explicitly state they were not very good. Upon passing the personal narrative, sportswriters must then distance themselves from fake Asian Lin-bandwagon basketball fans. Bringing up the flaws in Lin's game, ranking other pro point guards ahead of him, and questioning other Asian Americans' knowledge of the game are all acceptable tactics. Racism must not be mentioned unless it's to talk about how people only like Jeremy Lin because he's Asian. Failure to adhere to these regulations will result in Asian Americans being demoted back to table tennis.

Frank's Nursery and Crafts

The lines are long and my mom insists
that the final amount is wrong.
The cashier looks at the receipt and insists that it's right.
My mom purses her lips, looks worried,
says, *it's not right.*
The line of white people behind us groans.
My mom won't look back at them.
We both know what they're thinking.
Small woman with no knowledge of the way
things are in America.
Though year after year
she makes flowers bloom in the hood,
petals in the face of this land
that doesn't want her here.
Finally a manager comes, checks, and tells the cashier
she rang up twenty-two plants instead of just two,
overcharging us by forty dollars.
My mother holds my hand,
leads me away
without looking back
at the line of white people
who overhear
and gasp,
their sympathy won.
If only I was old enough
to tell them to keep it;
it's not my mom's English
that is broken.

"Allies" Who Think They're the Chosen Ones

Some dudes front like they're the Harry Potter of antiracism
when really
they're just trying
to Cho your Chang.

Are People of Color as Bad or Who's Bad or Bad Meaning Good

Like do you mean bad meaning good or bad meaning bad like genocide and slavery and using rifles as cocks or do you mean bad like *bad* bad but so bad we love you anyway like having a thing for bad boys like a phase of bad or are we talking bad to the scorched bone or like Darth Vader bad until the man asks you to fry your son or bad like a burning cross through a stained glass window bad or bad like a stabbing during a picnic on a perfect day bad or do you mean like bad but no get out of jail free card bad or do you mean bad credit bad or bad like two Asians in a room and they'll smile at everyone except each other bad or do you mean bad but let's do a study on why you're so bad or bad like bad phở (like unforgivably bad) or do you mean bad like racist against the Japanese imperialists for rape bad or do you mean bad because when history is so bloody there is no such thing as a mirror bad like when you need good so bad even bad a little is bad too much

Bad Driver, or Asian American Activists Who Talk about Their Own People Like They Are "Other"

Driving down a one-way street,
the Asian driver says Asians are the worst drivers
and they mean
the other Asian drivers
and not themselves
from inside a glass box,
air-conditioning in the summer,
heat in the winter,
doors
autolocked.
The Asian includes him- or herself as a bad driver in the hopes
that others think this makes them
a good driver.
The heated leather seats,
the premium trim,
the robot that tells them
they are going the right way.

They pass other Asians who
can't afford as nice a car or
risk getting pulled over or
have trouble reading the guide book or
can't read the language on the signs or
don't even have insurance or
their license is expired so they are scared
to drive too fast or
their cousin got pulled over once and
beaten down by the cops or
a cop pulled a gun on
them and said something about you people and war
and no one heard about it but
the Asian who wants to be seen
as the good driver

who was born
with
cruise control
zooms right by
on that one-way street
they are not talking
to the other Asians
the only time
they need to make
eye contact
with the people
they are talking about
and for
is when
they are
passing them
by

It Was Flame

Slavery
indentured servitude
migrant labor
genocide to clear land for theft
minimum wage so low
we can't see the ceiling:
America has been in business.

Shackle to sow.
Smallpox to blanket.
Guns bristle the border.
Lighter kisses hooch,
and how many times will you burn down Chinatown,
or whatever enclave we have been forced into,
to manifest your destiny.

One Black life would be one too many
and yet the police
multiply the number of murders nightly
as they have for
hundreds of years.
Teach me the
English
meaning of these words:
fair
justice
equity
as our bodies
are demarcated
by the light of our own
burning history.

They sang that it was wind blowing majestic across this nation—
    really it was flame.

Oriental Flavor

Oriental flavor must be a sidekick flavor / tastes like the margin not the center / tastes like an ally not the masses / tastes like napalm on a belly dancer / tastes like conical hats and flip-flops sweeping under trees riddled with bullet holes / tastes like overfished sushi and tears shed over killing dolphins / tastes like crushes on sushi waitresses / tastes like go back to where you came from / tastes like inverted phở fetish / tastes like fresh off the boat, straight into the housing projects / tastes like fiber-optic flowers in rotating glass cases / tastes like stabbings at Cedar Square / tastes like Aqua Net mist in New Wave hair / tastes like fish pulled out of mucky ponds by the highway for dinner / tastes like eight-hour perfume vapor in a sweatshop / tastes like a cop racially profiling Hmong / Cambodian / Pacific Islanders / Vietnamese / Chinese / Black / Indian / Latinx people / and on / and on / tastes like rust on a cell key thrown into a forgotten corner / tastes like the rust on a pirate blade / tastes like tears on a two-year-old toddler from a flashbang in a DEA raid / tastes like chinksweat from one who can dunk prime time and is called overrated / tastes like the middle of the crosshairs of a drone bomber / tastes like science concocting survival / tasteless until a new region of the tongue is discovered / dry until reconstituted with hot water / demonized spice packet / on whose tongue / can you taste hunger / for affordable resistance

Token Exceptional Asian in Liberal Multiculturalism

Sliver of gold
chink-narrow
swimming in a rainbow stream.
Are you the shiniest of the school
or are you bait?

At Dinner

In Vietnamese:
They put salt from the sea on chocolate now!

Sudden as a dip in a wave,
tones in the language
all hats and heavy dots and slashes up or down,
intuitively rising and falling,
how the Americans,
keeping track,
dropped their clipboards once the mortar shells started raining.
In the chaos,
who slipped onto the planes,
who got left behind.
Laughter about almost dying.
Small pauses,
a breath of empty space
for those who did.

Any one of my family
could walk down the street,
and suddenly
ching chong ching chong wah wah go back to where you came from,
or some sudden fist,
seeking a jaw
taught to sing our words
to make sense.
English slurs straightforward as bullets
that pierce, that leave
smoke and holes,
without once even considering
what we have survived.

Our language like a bubbling brook,
they say
you, Bao—you were three months old, but you were the least scared—
        you didn't cry, didn't make a single noise.
The world exploding all around a quiet baby,
grown up to be a man afraid of everything.

April 30, 2014

Second birthday
for our people

both sides:
loss started
long before.

One side can say
we were left alive,
but with nothing that made us *us*.

The other side says
they bombed us
to the beat of the sexiest music.

a girl running, on fire:
this didn't happen to you
but you can still feel the skin peeling
from your back.

(Others see history. You see a facsimile of your daughter.)

To say the past is past is bloodless privilege.

Malls now,
maybe bowling alleys,
maybe KFC.

High-rise hotels' lights pockmark the night
an electric rash.
Modernization is a clueless boyfriend.

Shells that speak in tones of "almost." Bombs leave craters that become tiny rice paddies. Machetes flash from the taxis. Post-traumatic stress muscles out in domestic violence, rape. Death shaking and choking in sleep. Too many mopeds going too fast, and not enough traffic, lights blink the colors of law.

And here you thought you were just a symbol of war.
You were a collection of near misses all along.

Apple-Red Pathfinder

He finally gets in and first thinks he's gone blind.
Sees nothing but a blanket of white.

A sign: maybe he should stop doing this.

The screwdriver in his hand,
a threat to the neck
of the steering column.
The Pathfinder
red in the snow,
an apple
dropped out of season.

His dad told him that everyone eats apples in this country.
They even have a rhyming slogan about it in their language.
So Dad tried to keep apples on the table,
to remind them who they should be.
This boy is from Vietnam, or Laos, or Cambodia,
does not speak the language most assume is his home tongue.
He imagines being a superhero who can see the future,
every action setting off a chain of possibility and consequence:
a missed bus saves a traveler late to the gas-station job
moments earlier sprayed with bullets by an armed robber.
Bumping into a crush at the mall leads to a date,
to marriage and kids, a house in the suburbs.

In a few minutes, this boy
will run in the snow under streetlamps that briefly illuminate
the skin of his origin,
with the screwdriver the police will swear looked like a pistol.
There will be popping noises that sound like the opposite of a celebration,
the lead heads of the bullets flattening, depending
on where they enter his body.

Now, he realizes his blindness is snow on a windshield.
The lightest breeze turns the powder to diamonds
under the streetlight.
Winter is as beautiful as every flake of snow,
coaxed to single crystals
until they pile back into an unknowable mountain.

No Question

*—To the white girl who saw a bunch of us little Southeast Asian kids
watching her brother play a video game in the Asian grocery and said,
"These gooks are surrounding us."*

Did we douse you in chemicals
that twisted your future generations
to flesh pretzels,
strip-mine your resources,
then fusion-fuck your family dinner

Did we light garlands of fire onto your sacred mountains,
push your people to tiny fingers of dry land,
explore what was already found,
then name your beautiful landmarks
after ourselves

Did we push your people into jobs
where toxic fumes turned your lungs into scorched wings,
your nails breaking on our skin
to paint ours pretty

Did we spin your history to smoke,
hook you on snorting the ashes

Did we convince the entire world your men
have cocks as small as minnows
scar barbed-wire borders using plastic surgery
break your legs to
make you
taller

Did we gentrify your love life

Did we convince your people
that we taught them the word *love*
and what it means to be free

Did we redefine torture
for our own benefit

Did we measure ourselves in fathoms
then force you to swim in us
until you drowned?

These gooks are surrounding us.
If only
that were true.

Villain/elle: Shimomura Cross Over in the Flat of the Night

—A villanelle regarding Shimomura Crossing the Delaware *by Roger Shimomura, after Dylan Thomas and Lupe Fiasco*

Shimo' cross over in the flat of the night
Home of the coolie, displaced Native, land of the slave
Paddle over tongues of water, Colonialist's Delight.

Tie an Arab to a rocket, set the fuse alight
Enlist a Chinaman in the military, racists haze the brave
Shimo' cross over in the flat of the night.

Steal Native land, dance the white man's blight
Drop bombs on Jap, teach yellows to behave
Paddle over tongues of water, Colonialist's Delight.

Shackle woman, shackle man, pack them in tight
You can never get enough, what a white man craves—
Shimo' cross over in the flat of the night

Build a wall against a people, barbwire their flight
Natives declared illegal, upturned sacred graves
Paddle over tongues of water, Colonialist's Delight.

Indian accent over phone lines, xenophobia our birthright
We fight over scraps, these holes onto our souls engraved
Shimo' cross over in the flat of the night
Paddle over tongues of water, Colonialist's Delight.

Rolling through a Four-Way

9:35 a.m. on a bright day on the way to day care one cop is positioned
behind the wheel back on the side where your toddler dark hair yellow
skin like a burst of a reverse sunflower sits strapped into her booster seat a
hand on his gun elbow cocked a scarecrow angle do I make myself as small
a target as possible as my people have learned to do in this country will it
save me will my daughter see me handcuffed or shot when I reach for the
insurance information will I blame the closest person to me will I blame
myself who will blame me who will say I have no right to say anything on
the other side of the horizon of glass the police officer asks you to roll your
window down his claw on the butt of his gun standing as if shielding the
whiteness of his hand against the matte black gun but you can see it the
other cop's gun in the mirror too both closer than they appear

Bầu Cua Cá Cọp

—*With thanks to Sahra Nguyen for the refugee-style slogan*

After the martial arts and the dancers and the bamboo xylophone
they bring out the board for bầu cua cá cọp.
To save money, my dad made our board,
used a soup bowl to trace the six large circles,
drew the fish, prawn, crab, rooster, calabash, and stag himself.
The heavy white dice he had to buy,
as if to taunt his hypocrisy:
making a gambling game at the same time as telling us to save money.
The same reason he only gave me two quarters to blow at Thompson's
    Arcade.

What he never had to say:
Waste what you got
pretty soon
you'll waste what you don't got, too.

They give the kids candy to bet.
My daughter loses the first four rounds;
she's a quiet wire as they take her candy away, piece by piece.
When she finally wins, I ask if she wants to play again.
No! she shouts, grabbing her candy, *I want to go home!*
True refugee style: *Take everything you got and run with it.*

58

II.

Future Letter to Daughter Apologizing for When I Caved to Her Request and Brought Her to Barbie's Dreamhouse at Mall of America

So many times I wish I were stronger.

Everybody needs a Ken,
the song chirps on repeat.
Already I walk where I don't exist.

You propelled yourself, wobbly cannonball,
down bruise-colored hallways,
not acting ladylike at all,
ignored the preening at the makeup stations
to jump spasmodically in place,
wanted to bake pretend cupcakes in the fake ovens
so you could eat them all yourself.

Still.
How can I teach you not to ask for the pink cars,
the thin threads,
the hierarchy of blondes,
the sell to be skinny
without your wanting it all anyway?

I can't promise I'd write a poem
if you were a boy
jumping boots first into a G.I. Joe land,
staring down the eyes of cannons that shoot
but never kill.

In the end, whose resistance will you take on?

Love that gives my life meaning,
so beautiful I can scarce believe you're cast from me at all—
I am so sorry
for the plastic worlds I helped bring you into.

Broken Things

Let's call him O.
He was loud,   .
wore his hair long,
wore all black,
banged his head,
gave zero fucks before giving zero fucks was a thing.
O. was an Asian but a bad Asian, but then again back then there were
      only bad Asians
so that shit was redundant to everyone but us.
His given name he never told us
said we couldn't pronounce it anyway.
The whispers said:
we should be nice to him cuz his daddy beats him.
O. turned his arm upside down once
to show burn scars shaped like cigarettes—
then winked at me.
O. made life hell for almost everyone except for me—
looked at me the way a pit bull who has decided to defend kittens might.
Those times I would want to ask him more but didn't.
One night O. found a lightbulb in a dead lot in the dark
threw it so hard that that burnt-out bulb spun end over end
'til it met something harder than itself and broke.
Before the end of its ellipse we were running
short fits of breath puffing
O. making monster noises.
He could not see if I was laughing or crying
in the dark.

Decades later I travel and read poems,
thankful to strangers
who like me because they don't know me yet.
Kids once bullied by kids like O.
have grown up to create avant-garde hot dog bars,

wax their mustaches,
drink shit you can't even pronounce.

O., we assume his story is sad because it started that way.

True story: two Japanese men scuba dive for a wife, a daughter,
lost five years ago to a tsunami.
They dive, and they dive, and they dive again,
trying to find a place beyond hope.
They are at their best
when the ones they love
can't see.

We're talking about O., of course,
how none of us can predict
even what we know.

And what of the kitten?
Well let's just say
if you are a parent
yet the one thing that might make you special is that you are a poet—
God help you.

I've realized that I yell the same things to my daughter
in the same way that my dad would yell at me
except I do it in English
which some may consider the official language
of bad Asians.
The apartment building has several single-parent families like ours—
we know the juggling of a foot to catch a door,
one hand carrying groceries,
the other a bag of toys the child has refused to hold,
children wanting us to sprout a third arm
to carry them over the threshold.
We say the same thing to their spread and hopeful arms

in three different languages
not knowing if it's us or some god when we say
I can't carry you.

What if this is the best we can be?
When we realize phrases like "Be who you were meant to be"
make no sense at all.

Look into a burnt-out lightbulb,
see that something that should lead to something else
is broken.

Document

I.

Let's say the smart white girl from the wealthy family that you always thought was so pretty ends up being part of your study group, and she comes to your house with the others to work on the final project. She wrinkles her nose and asks if there are roaches, and instead of hating her you hate your mom and dad. She'll never love you, but that's preferable to their love, which you've grown to need a translator for. They taught you you were ugly long before this white girl caught your eye. They are nowhere near to hear her English; they're off at one of their two or three jobs. You've learned about the Black Panthers in a gym room closet, you've learned about the AIM patrols in your neighborhood, but you don't know how it all connects to crushes balanced atop nests of roaches. Don't know what to do with these feelings but tuck it all away and hope it doesn't crawl out like it will at sudden moments for the rest of your life. Can't seem to figure out what all of that has to do with your war-torn family and this beautiful woman who hates the house you're raised in, its scuttling denizens. Whether or not they're real, she imagines you infesting this place.

II.

In my twenties, my body is bloated from overeating and I don't know what to believe in that will make me happy, so of course I am getting porn. I am so scared someone will recognize me and force me to erase my name from every radical leftist petition I've ever signed. I start to pull out of the small parking lot when two white men in a big American truck pull in at the same time, swerving it in and blocking my way like that American-made tonnage is their dick. They're taller than me, in their truck and also on foot, I can tell. I throw my hands up and roll my eyes, then as I back my car to get out of their way, one of the white men unbuckles his seat belt, threatening that he will jump out and kick my ass. Then he and his friend laugh at me, that laugh of superiority that you don't even need to hear the noise to recognize: "Look, we played chicken with this chink, and we won." Here's the part where I say I went home and whacked off while fantasizing about having sex with his girlfriend, but that's not true. Instead I stored the memory away and now it eats at me every time someone says they think I'm a great guy.

III.

I lied about my age so I could work at the supermarket pushing carts and cutting apart cardboard boxes with a razor, the triangle of its sharp head encased in a white metal sleeve. I am really sixteen when I am walking parallel to the train tracks on the back end of Minnehaha, back toward Phillips, trying to find a path through the snow. A car whips past, window open, a voice yells CHINK. FUCK YOU, I shout back into the whip of the dark. The tires squeal and a white boy jumps out, pushes me down. I recall he called me a gook and a faggot, too. I get up and slide my hand into my pocket, the metal cold, silent as I push the blade out, which promises to extend my reach. A pretty white girl is pleading from the passenger seat for him to leave me alone. *He's a fucking asshole,* she explains to me, as if that explained everything. Bless her anyway. I don't know if it's for her or my fear of potential police that keeps my hand, curled around a sharp promise, behind my back. In all the books I love, the hero doesn't strike first. But then again, none of the heroes look like me. In a few minutes, I'll walk home, unbruised but defeated, and ask my oldest brother for a gun. I don't explain why. He nods, but he never gets me one. Out of all of us, he remembers the war the most. He knows all about promises we can't keep.

IV.

It's not a majority-white school. In seventh grade, the tall blond tomboy asks you to dance. You have no idea all the boys have a crush on her; you've been busy with comic books, and the only romance you know are tragedies from Greek mythology and Arthurian legends. She's your best friend and you've laughed together every day, so of course you say yes. You're both smiling as you sway on the linoleum where, just moments before, you and other members of student council folded then cleared the lunchroom tables out for this DJ to play his slow jams in the dark. You laugh with her, as you always do, even when she puts her chin on your shoulder. Suddenly you notice three white boys looking at you two, snickering. They come right up to both of you, and whisper in her ear. Loud enough for you to hear. *Everyone can see you dancing with that gook,* they laugh. She responds by flicking them off, pulling you closer. Years later you'll wonder how she created her armor. *You know those gooks only want one thing from white girls,* another said. He's one of your best friends. To this day, when you think a woman just might, through whatever miracle, see any beauty in you, you can still hear them laughing through the cages of their teeth. The biggest fist you have is the one banging against the inside of your rib cage.

Lights

A small handle with fiber-optic cables springing like snakes from Medusa's head. Press a button and tiny colored dots at the end of the translucent strings would light. The day after the Shrine Circus, all the kids in my class had them, waving them. My dad asked me if he'd ever broken a promise, and I said nothing—he never took me to the circus because he didn't have the money, not because he couldn't keep a promise. How do you say that to your father. Almost thirty years later, my daughter and I go to the circus. First time for both of us. She holds my hand and wants to run past the bouncy castles, the face painting, the pony rides—all things she loves, all things that cost money. Sitting alone in our seats, waiting, I ask her why she doesn't want to be where everyone else is. Because I don't know if you can afford it, she whispers, then leans her head into my chest, and I am glad she can't see my face. Later—after the Orientals have been introduced and pretzel-thrown themselves into the thick air, the circus runners turn out the lights—over the loudspeaker some asshole will tell all the kids to lift their glowing butterfly wands, lightsabers, laser pistols into the air and wave them proudly, show them off, and tell us over and over that if we want one, if we really really want one, we can buy them from the men holding enormous bags lumbering up and down the aisles like mercenary Santas. The light-up things pulse, illuminating my daughter's face in hyphens of light as she stares across a sea of bright things, a thousand blinking promises never asked for, a thousand flashing neon signs telling her what she doesn't have.

In the Dark

When I first saw them, glass fuses looked like jewels.
Solid and sharp, rings of color to label wattage,
their weight in my small hands made them serious.
Grooved tails meant they belonged somewhere.

My dad decided it was time for me to learn—
along with how to breathe when shooting a gun,
holding two-by-fours for him to saw while he cursed
his lot in life—

I would trade these jewels for light.

I summoned the courage to ignore
my older siblings telling me murderers and monsters
lived in the sweated concrete of our basement.
With a book of matches I pretended I was a warrior,
torch in hand, the fuse box my treasure chest.

I kept some of the blown ones, smudged as if given black eyes,
and ran my fingers along their hard edges.
He's too young, he could get electrocuted, my mom protested.
If you didn't use the microwave and the grill at the same time,
we'd still have power, my dad would rebut.

While my parents debated who I'd grow up to be in this country
and my siblings imagined different locations for monsters,
I curled my fist around the fuses 'til the edges left lines in my palms.
These baubles exchanged for light.
Treasure paid for things I wasn't old enough to fix.

Careful What You Wish For

Seriously! Last night I had a dream that I was a white man. Unlike in my youth, when I fantasized about such things, this time I did not ask for it— and yet there I was in the mirror: high, sharp cheekbones; sensible but not-too-fussy hair; striking eyes; good facial hair. I decided to see how it went.

I wasn't particularly exceptional but my average was something everyone seemed impressed with. In cafés and bars and in big green open spaces I suddenly felt like a vortex instead of a stain. I felt like I would always find a way to take care of my daughter. I went back to college and strangely, I finally understood physics. I walked by classrooms and impressive buildings like they one day might be named after me. I stopped second- and third-guessing every decision I made or desire I had.

I took dance lessons, and my beautiful dance partner said, *You don't have to tell me you love me, I'll tell you I love you and always have.*

But we just met, I tried to say. *You don't know about . . .*

I don't care, she said, grabbing me and twirling around on the parquet like we were meant to orbit one another just so.

When I woke up from this dream, the first thing I said to myself was: "that dream was *not* your fault." And I repeated that, over and over.

Tourist with Daughter

I sit with our daughter at the top of the Space Needle,
eating hot dogs we paid tourist prices for.
It's fine, really, in this place high up, these assumptions
of who we are and what we can afford.

I want to tell our daughter that my dad could never afford
something like this for me.
But what good would that be.

I'm not using her name in this poem because
she hasn't given me permission.

When I was about six, my dad looked me in the eye
and challenged me to point out one time
he failed to keep a promise.
I thought then of half a dozen occasions but stayed silent.

I ask our daughter what she likes up here and she says
the clouds, and the boats.

From up this high you think you can see everything.
I'm amazed she likes sour corn syrup sticky candy more than a Kobe beef
    hot dog.

When she looks bored, I want to tell her that
we can't always have what we want.
When really, some of us can never have what we want.

But instead I stay silent,
look at the clouds and the boats
as if for the first time.

Contour

I know the contours of want: the board game about getting rich
from the thrift store, missing too many pieces to play
so I made up my own game.

My sparkly Tonka truck that Mom tried to sell at the garage sale.
The things new in boxes, sitting straight on store shelves,
hard-plastic blister a window to things we couldn't afford.
I would read the backs of the packages, commit the ethnicity of each
    G.I. Joe and his primary
and secondary specializations to memory,
firepower and speed of Optimus Prime versus Sideswipe.

My dad got a gun because that's what soldiers do,
even when they're not on the front lines.
Hid it, locked away
secret where I never found it;
watched two of his sons
join the U.S. military,
read the paper about war on his break.
He wanted more: just enough, but more,
for us.

I would run around the block, pretend I was running away from home
unable to see my way out of this place, all cracked concrete and broken
bottles and black swirls of graffiti I could read but not understand:
why people looked at us, called us names,
pushed us around like we had never survived anything.

I wanted to fight and fight and be this big person who'd make you tremble
just being near, wouldn't even need to hear me talk
to know I was important,
fear the trajectory of my fists and the orbit of my kicks.
You would hide, and then you would want
to be me

and none of the people I loved would ever want for anything
so of course they would want me.

Today my daughter likes Hello Kitty but I'm not convinced she sees it.
Vague shapes, no mouth,
thick outlines of symmetry and dots and flat planes of color,
blue and purple and pink,
looping lines forming empty shapes,
sparkle that has to be glued on, yet flakes off.
She orbits the shapes and tears at them for hours
until she falls asleep and forgets them.
I never know if she ever feels full within her own outline.

I fear I'm spoiling her.
Then I remember what family she comes from
and I think to myself
let her have,
and throw away.

Full Contact

Five-year-old brushes her teeth like it's a contact sport—
holds the toothbrush still inside her tense grimace, then
shakes her whole head vigorously.
She plays air guitar, moving her hands seemingly at random
but with a look of intense concentration,
afraid to miss a note.
All very Waverly.
Not just to combat stereotypes, I want to tell her
to swing an air-record scratch in there,
disrupt rock-goddess fantasy with that typewriter clack-spit
she claims is beatboxing.
Take a night off from flossing.
Love the toothpaste
that never made it to the walls of your teeth,
instead splattering to crust the sink.
There will be more than enough years
to punish yourself for imperfection.
Dream yourself a unicorn shitting rainbows
propelling you much higher
than gossamer wings.

Geek Triptych

I. *King of Monsters*

Whether due to a persona I developed in Phillips to avoid getting jumped, or the astral projection of introvert armor, or simply by virtue of being a Southeast Asian male in Minnesota, strangers usually don't try to talk to me. But maybe as I get older, I appear more welcoming. The other day a seemingly nice older white man whom I don't know exclaimed, "I really don't care for this hot weather—are you from Japan?" *Hell yeah,* I should have said. *In fact, you know that movie Godzilla? That's based on my life. Yet do you see them crediting me? I am sick of Hollywood co-opting my story. It makes me want to vomit radioactive apocalypse and commit zombie homicide, except in my version there's more than one Asian who survives.* Our real conversation was not nearly as fun, but at least it didn't end in violence. Our daughter overheard this and admonished me: "Don't talk to strangers, Daddy." It was a beautiful day outside, perfect for reading a new book in short-sleeved clothing, which I did, all the while reminding myself to scowl more in public.

II. *Capes*

I dreamed that I was a part of a hero team hopelessly overmatched by biological beings that could grow additional limbs and stretch at will to murder. Elastic monsters, they overcame our stagecoach. Then we asked what we were doing riding a stagecoach. Their leader was a blond white alpha male who looked like what would make him perfect would be if one of his brown followers died, and in so doing, taught him a valuable lesson about valuing life and humility and kindness. We heroes hid in darkness: cavernous, condemned buildings made romantic by their abandonment. We snuck, we observed, we cowered in fear, we took things out on each other. All seemed lost but then I slipped into that place between sleep and wakefulness just enough to give myself a lightsaber. Neuron by neuron I felt my body shift from the deep end of the dream toward consciousness. In the end I slew the bad guy, but I had to be awake to do it.

III. *Listening*

What if there was an X-Man whose mutant power was generating flaw-lessly, and at any volume, songs in their own head. They'd be weak against Sentinels but good for working out. Think of all the money she or he would save from buying records, iTunes, Beats by Dre headphones, and whatnot. Maybe they'd have the power to put music in other people's heads too, but sharing music you love is its own kind of selfishness. If I had that power I'd lie on my back on a boat floating around in some estuary, staring up at the stars, content to be my own jukebox.

Balsa Wood Free Association

Hardware stores sell airplanes
in thin plastic bags,
flat slats of balsa wood
that you jam together through pre-sawed grooves,
throw the entire flimsy thing into the air
and hope for flight.
My dad would sometimes buy one for me—
his hope, most likely, to seed ambition
to be an engineer,
or even a pilot,
some well-paying job
that would eradicate my need
to visit hardware stores in the future.
It didn't work.
I didn't pay attention when I held two-by-fours for my dad to saw.
I couldn't stop picturing my hands getting cut off in some accident.
So now I'm old and I can't fix a thing.
The only time I have felt beautiful
is when I've had the chance to sit still
looking at a body of water and stone,
waves crashing or currents rolling
around jagged edges that have no plan
but to be worn down—
hard formations I could not possibly survive
if I landed on them.

For All Heartbroken Pizza Delivery Boys

She did it over a landline.
We still had those back then.
I thought we would lead Asian America to a revolution together—
I was very wrong.
Eventually I put on my dark-green polo shirt with *Davanni's* stitched over
the half-baked remains of my heart
and went on my routes,
the incomprehensible roads of Prospect Park
like a snake eating itself in the shadow of a witch's hat.
No one could tell I was having nervous breakdowns
from pizza to pizza.
It never affected the tipping,
which was universally shitty.
The cardboard boxes trapped heat and protected cheese and pepperoni
    alike
from my tears.
Seriously.
I did not believe there would ever be a reason to love life.
I couldn't see, years later, that I'd be typing poems
on this thing called Facebook during my lunch break,
missing my hilarious daughter
not too far from that pizza franchise
where the supervisor asked me during my job interview
why I wanted to work there and I drew a blank—
to deliver pizza?
Are all questions doomed to be so existential?
Some dude tried to rob me on Cedar Avenue.
I told him,
go ahead,
shoot,
fuck you.

His eyes were glazed, as confused as I was
about why we were both
on that street,
at that time,
being who we needed to be.

Theresa, I Think

In grade school there was a sweet, quiet girl who loved Prince. She cried every time she heard "Purple Rain," and she would listen to it a lot. Maybe you can't trust the memory of a poet who can't remember if it was fourth or fifth or sixth grade, but I recall that we asked her once why and she couldn't explain. If I had known then what I know now, I would have offered that a guitar solo can be made of guts and can gut you, all at once. That unlike our throats, when our hearts howl they never grow hoarse. That a raindrop can weep inside of itself so hard it drowns and, looking at it, you would never know.

Incomplete / Abridged

I.
Another city. Her city. Her black hair
has gotten long, to her shoulders.
You're yoked to her eyebrows.
She's going to change the world for the better.
But not with you.
On this night
for whatever reason
she slips her arm through yours.
We look good together, she says.
She tilts her head to rest on your head,
and it becomes everything—
it doesn't matter that it will go
nowhere.
Right then we are everything.

II.
They play a game at work.
Between orders for no cilantro,
black beans or pinto.
On the other side of the gentrifying line
between kitchen and the front of the house
marked by swinging doors,
the cute waitstaff decides to play a game: who at work is the sexiest?
One of the white men thought it up,
because he wants the friendly, gorgeous blonde to say his name.
Instead she says mine.
No one expects it.
I'm in the kitchen—
far away from the game,
the one no one's slept with.
She never touches me.
I never expect her to.
She becomes this chink's saint.

III.
No long distance. No vegans. No Asians.
No addicts. No Christians.
Who do you break your own laws for?

IV.
Tattoos & tongue kisses & piercings & ecstasy
she pulls you in with both her arms
becomes all lips and tongue
you can do nothing
but be pulled
to where you will stay—
she'll be the one
that leaves.

V.
I had a dream that I was living in a square alcove in front of an elevator.
The elevator itself was broken, permanently open,
but I didn't want to risk living in a box
that could suddenly lurch closed, then up or down.
There wasn't much to that space, but it was mine.
In the dream, an Asian American woman, whom I once loved
and therefore always will,
visited me often, and we both wondered if she could love me back.
We kept wondering.
I walked the dream streets and the concrete felt solid enough,
the night's neon was inviting, the fast food familiar.
No one asked me where I was really from.

VI.
Because my brain
likes to punch down
on my
heart

VII.

Joke that when we are together,
they see a terrorist and a little-dick footbinder
holding hands, and can only imagine
what explosions and negotiations are held hostage between you.
What flag you fly when you kiss.
What borders crossed.
In the end it's you on a Chinatown bus
going nowhere but away—
no sand, no jungle,
no napalm, no nuke,
smoke from the exhaust like a fizzled fuse.

VIII.

She asks you out to a bar and wants to know
what it feels like to be an Asian man,
invisible, taught to believe in our own unattractiveness.
So you tell her, but then she grabs you by the collar
and yanks you across the table to her lips,
kisses you in front of everyone so hard
the paradigms shift.
It is the best way anyone has ever shut you up.

IX.

The only one who wrote you poems.
Her lips drag on you, roads
you will remember.
You begged. She acquiesces.
You become
one another's favorite secret,
again and again.
You beg.
She becomes God.

X.
She's locked you both out of her place.
It's raining, you're sitting in her car,
she's singing to you.
Singing to you.
She closes her eyes to let you know
that this song is loss,
and she smiles
as her voice finds the tributaries
in breath, hitches around the notes—
the drops of rain
wander down the glass
and become rivers wherever they go.
She'll break your heart, but not
in this moment.

XI.
You're just not attracted to Asian men?
It's okay.
I'm not attracted to racism.

XII.
It's so simple it hurts—
in the dream she wants you.
Gets on a plane, plays Jenga with her schedule,
say yes—
you are worth this good work.
Of course you are grateful; her smile is accurate
to the crease,
even in the haze of your REM.
She looks at you the whole time,
her hand in yours
and she sees everything.

Epilogue.
Disappear into a history
you break your own heart to write.

Therapist 4

A river, wanting to go downhill
will carve new tributaries,
tear through homes,
flood the roots of trees.
The therapist tells you your mind
is swollen with doom
that carries you in its white rush,
torrents ripping through
rock and root.

I don't know in what direction love pulls me.
But I do know the feeling of the muscle in your chest flailing
for fear of drowning.

At Minnehaha, a young Southeast Asian couple asked me
to take their picture.
Cambodian, or Lao, or Thai, or Viet.
He was heavily tattooed and looked like the dudes
who would have whooped my ass just for breathing,
back in the day.
She had dyed hair,
looked like the girls who dismissed me
as a pasty, boring little sellout back then.
They're the most gorgeous couple in the park.
If it sounds like I'm making assumptions about them and me,
I am,
and it's not okay
just because I'm Asian too.

They like the picture I take for them.
The creek and the falls are swollen from the rains.
The same that have deluged basements,
dips in the road,
drowned park benches too close to the lake shore.

Each raindrop doesn't care
if it's the one to soak in
or the one that stays above it all to flood.
They just throw themselves on top of each other
until they become bigger than who they were
when they were apart.

Chess Pride, Waverly Style

The funny thing is the local alt-weekly
mostly black and white
does a Valentine's issue,
wants you to be a part of a *how they met* article.
Finally!
An Asian American couple will be featured,
you think.
Too bad you broke up three weeks ago.
Should we do our duty for the race?
Get our faces, if not our hearts, in the paper?
Take it seriously.
What if the picture
is in color?

Night of the Living

I.

There are places that were once places,
overgrown now. You can imagine lighting
a small fire amid moss-covered stone walls.
Motivational posters of eagles and canyons long since faded.
Eating jerky, holding a pistol and looking out
for danger outside the dome of warmth.
But really, once those places are given over they are done.
The comfort from the knowledge no security guard will remove you
only goes so far. You'll start to wonder if another's voice
would sound good in the dark echo.
If eyes reflected across the fire
could make you forget the existence of coffee.
Solitude is different from loneliness.
The abandoned places in the world know this.

II.

Edible-Seaweed Broadside in the Hour of Chaos:

I read that sea lettuce (*Ulva lactuca*) and dulse (*Palmaria palmata*) are
    preferred.
Wash thoroughly of sand,
and the microscopic jewelry of small shells clinging in the folds.
Bilious green popped balloons hung to dry.
Press into brittle sheets.
For edible ink, reduce over a fire:
prune juice, red wine, beet juice, or concord grape juice
(samurai, katana, haiku—already reduced).
But what color will show up on such a broken green?
Matching the pallor of zombies, who shuffle broken and irregular
as if on the ends of puppeteer strings.
The alphas, meaning hunters, stalking rabbit and deer,
and the gatherers, plucking herbs and scavenging hygiene products,
they could read the poems printed on the roasted seaweed sheets
then eat.

A notebook of them in a pack:
lightweight, and light.
Providing protein, iodine, umami.

Maybe the useful would ponder the words,
then consume
and we would all stop,
even if for a moment,
asking what good poetry is
words perforated on such a brittle cloud that could be eaten:
stained glass already shattered.

III.
In my dreams I am granted powers to slay,
put down the dead
the way some would plant rice—
alpha male without the attitude
or entitlement—
I just want to help, I'd say.
My family would be in some far, safe place
as part of an agreement for my superheroics.
And a beautiful woman would love me
because of my humble asskickery.
You're different, not like Chase or Donovan at all!
she'd say in admiration.
I'd pick wildflowers
and not just hygiene products,
would load a gun without it being about my penis.

As a little boy it was silver-plated armor
my dad made from foil and cardboard
and a sword with a name,
a towel for a cape,
flashlight for a lightsaber,
toilet paper tubes taped into the shape of a blaster.

I've always dreamed so far away from who I am.

Tonight I want to close the book on my need.
If there were a zombie apocalypse I could tell you
the best rock to sit on to see the stars,
since there would be no light pollution.
I'd salvage books, save the stale Kit Kats for when the woman I have a
    crush on
had a bad day.
Unconditional love,
I wouldn't have scavenged any condoms
because my giving is pure.

But I don't want to be useful—
tonight I will see
if dreaming of being myself
is ever going to be enough.

IV.

Your therapist knew this day would come. She knows you had to get over
your once-blatant-then-unconscious belief that therapy is for privileged
white people. To her credit she never told you *get over yourself or die.* She
sometimes looks at you like a sweater sprouting a bunch of frayed threads
that she wants to pull on. How do I help raise an Asian child in a country
with a political right that will hate her unless she assimilates and they can
use her, and a radical left that will hate her unless she assimilates and they
can use her? Yes, I survived, and you'd think I feel good about that but
I don't. You know my parents don't have internet? They don't even have
computers. Don't feel sorry for them—they probably hate you and are
talking shit about you in Viet, hoping you don't understand. I'm talking
to you, reader, and not my therapist. They don't need Twitter or Facebook for
that. When and if the wicked come for my family and my loved ones, I will
not have the power to do anything. All this shouting will not have helped
anyone. And yet my first reaction *not* being simply to punch people I dis-
like in the face is a type of progress? Zombie apocalypse scenarios make
you ponder the practical application of who you are and what you believe.

Okay, your therapist says, *so you may not have the skill set that would allow you to do backflips and chop off three zombie heads at once—my challenge to you is to think about and value how you, the real you, could contribute, and think about if you already are contributing to the world and your loved ones.* Well that's no fun, you think, but your therapist is always right about you. So last night, instead of dreaming that you were a hero with violent alpha-male abilities but with a nerd sensibility, like some type of gook Captain America, you imagined—in the middle of jump scares and zombie beheadings and hot desperate people fucking each other—a building with a Linotype machine and abandoned reams of paper and gallons of ink. You could create small messages to let people know they weren't alone, or crush notes for the crush-ons, or shit-talking missives to people you dislike. And it would mean something, because you might have used the very last ink and paper in the world to love, lift, or hate. If there were a zombie apocalypse and you sat in a place where all the potential stories and poems and love letters and arguments were just waiting for a brain and a heart and a hand, it wouldn't matter if it was fate or luck or destiny. You wouldn't sit there wondering what you're good for.

Mouse

There is a mouse who comes out from under the fridge at exactly midnight. I go to sleep early but these days I've been burning the midnight oil trying to write new poems, getting discouraged and becoming convinced I have no talent, and then watching *Game of Thrones*. The mouse seems deeply disappointed that I am awake, then scurries away. Mouse, I don't know what you want from me—that's why your opinion matters so much! *You're a better being than me, I'm sure of it,* I want to say. My therapist told me, *Your problem may be that you give too many fucks,* and observed that I am able to see nuance and challenge binary / dichotomous thinking concerning race, but not when I am judging myself. Am I a good dad or a bad dad? Am I beautiful or not? Am I good overall or bad overall? Am I useful or not? A bad poet or a good poet? Do I deserve to be alive or not? And so on. I keep having these dreams where I'm left behind, and when I wake up I feel like I deserve to be alone. Mouse, when you creep out from under the place I must assume you've always known, what do you see? Someone who is doing his best, and if you are patient, you get what he gets? Or someone who simply inhabits a space you'd rather have all to yourself? I am trying to see things your way. There are all these little spaces that make us into who we are, and sometimes I can't breathe when I feel stuck. I think of stars and ocean waves, mouse: these things that are bigger than me and can't be bothered to care.

For Brandon Lacy Campos

I.

I had this dream that the world was ending in a week. Instead of flipping out, there were giant free festivals all over the world where people could spend time with friends and family; even some peeps who had passed on came back from the dead to party. There were free workshops, concerts, and activities for people so they could learn and participate in things they never got a chance to do. I took a workshop on miniatures painting and elaborate diorama creation. I went with some friends to an open mic and heckled this poet. I realized he was a stand-in for everyone who ever dissed me and thought I was too dumb to realize it. FUCK Y'ALL, FUCK Y'ALL, I kept shouting at him. I didn't care if I deserved to be so mean; it just felt good not having to pretend anymore. There was an activity where you had to escape from a room that was set up like a puzzle—I had to roll into a ball like Samus to get out.

When I did, Brandon was outside the room on a cobblestone street, a drink in his hand, chatting with J. and a bunch of other friends. He winked at me and said, *Don't worry, I've been having too much fun in the afterlife to waste my time judging you from afar. Let's party! And I'm glad I finally get to meet Song.*

II.

Wherever you are now, may the only poems needed spill from the breath of angels. May the winks and the drinks be made of cloud. May the People of Color soccer leagues be free of drama. May the marches call you and all the lost into the streets for a collective embodiment of the fabulous. May there never be another prison, not even the ones we make for ourselves. Love to you brother. Love to you most of all.

Well Then

—After Agha Shahid Ali

There's no explaining it away.
I may as well tell myself
the wind never cradled a rough sheet on a ragged line.
Or that a wave
could not carry wood,
worn through by the hunger of worms
back to a shore that reminded it of home.
I may as well deny that stars
are fuel, long in coming and long in staying.
But it's no use.
Here I am again, thinking of you and hoping
that in you, I beat like a raindrop,
or a favorite song, or that I drum
in a dream,
unfold like a pillow
a vague shape,
to exist somewhere
in your landscape—
that you hold me
not caring
about the estimation of my worth
but that I am solid
in your arms
to beat the small histories
that we allow to hold us back
and away—
let us write
as if the world were paper
and we our own stories
to live tell.

In Harbor

You've never been good at doing more
than one thing at once,
but you're learning.
So you listen, every time you listen,
whether or not you were meant to understand,
her voice a bell calling ships to harbor
you tell yourself
friends are friends and friends are good
and
be cool
and
be patient
and
no expectations.
Some of these stories sail slowly
as if every small town were made of stories
unfolding,
a lake needing storm clouds
so you listen and you listen and you don't know
who is who but maybe a harbor
is a sort of story that stands still—
how could she swallow a waterfall
then learn to speak through rain.
Stories so vast
that the ocean swallows the horizon and
we are all just silhouettes
against a sun, and even the sun must surrender
if even for just a little while
and that is beautiful.
You wonder if you can ask the moon
to be an ache in your doorframe twice.
You wonder if the flap of a butterfly's wings in China
will sway her just a step back toward you.
You wonder if the stars and magic will ever be on your side.

You see her again but this time it's her door.
She invites you in,
her smile both harbor and storm
and you feel like a boat
made of nervous birds.
She asks, can I tell you a story?
Yes and yes and yes and yes.

III.

Ego-Tripping as Self-Defense Mechanism for Refugee Kids Who Got Their Names Clowned On

My given name, Thiên-bảo,
translates to
treasure from heaven.
An immediate reason for my being
indecipherable
the moment it stung
unfamiliar tongue
so soon after "hello."
I would finally like to thank my parents
for what I once thought of
as an unpronounceable curse
that I'd have loved to bleach—
because everyone who has ever addressed me
from bullies to crushes to haters
has had no choice
but to call me
valuable.

Not a Silverfish

A large centipede was in my tub for days.
It looked like a prehistoric zipper made of needles.
A firecracker with too many fuses.
I skipped taking a shower for far too long—
an unspoken compromise—hoping
it would disappear on its own,
preferring to be dirty over drowning my fear.
Eventually I trapped it in a container,
took it outside while it scrambled
like an explosion of exclamation points
in the foggy plastic,
and let it go.
These centipedes are often mistaken for silverfish—
they actually make dinner of them
and other more damaging pests.
I know what it's like to be mistaken for something else,
to feel that the first reaction when a new set of eyes encounters your body
is to want to smash you.
To wonder what in history made a caterpillar a caterpillar,
a ladybug a ladybug.
To know what it's like to be invisible until revealed to be ugly,
alien thing, hairy wiggle
whose body tells the only story
anyone is willing to hear.
When it shook free of my trap,
its head made of stepladders,
its body a spasm of a hundred loose threads of fate,
it didn't make a sound but I swear
I could hear it scream that it wanted
to travel to prehistory
and rewrite the many veins of possibility
that would shape how it would be seen

so that the present could be a place
where it could be
understood for what
it was.

Being Asian in America

Survive long enough
and eventually
everything becomes
a revolution.

Untitled / Fathers

The fathers I know don't name their children after themselves.
Bodies of water never still,
teachers without a name,
colors too deep for the human eye to translate,
a street curving off in both directions,
a country spirit whose voice is a bell in the wind—
we give names to things that cannot be contained or restrained,
even naming them minimizes them.

Names in languages that must be sung but that we can barely speak.

We look into our children's faces and see the end of all we know.
All our lives we have been made to feel small and now at last
this is a good thing.

One day I'll say I want to give you everything because I come from not so much
and no matter how far away I get I feel too close to nothing every day.

Maybe the important thing is that you made me realize I just want a
    better world for you to be a small part of.

The moment you were born you were better than me.

Every moment after that is to be determined.

Thousand Star Hotel

Vietnamese people joke that they don't need a four-star hotel—even the homeless, sleeping in the wide open, are treated to a thousand star hotel every night. 1996 in the countryside of Vietnam, I front like I'm better than a tourist simply because I was born here. Hot-spring water is piped into a spartan concrete pool, so gray you can tell its color in the pitch dark. Overhead are the most stars I've ever seen in my life. They take what little breath I have away. The night is so deep and gorgeous without the light. I can't swim, not even to save myself, but still I soak and look overhead. I am self-conscious because my body is rail thin and pale. I am frustrated because the hot water fogs up my glasses constantly. I curse my bad luck, my bad eyesight. What I should have done is kept wiping, and kept gazing, if only for a second at a time. Because luck is returning to a homeland you are too young to embody. Because you never know if you'll get a second chance to be a witness to beauty. Because stars don't care about inconvenience; their gorgeousness took an eternity to reach us and they have done the work and are worth it. So wipe away. See what your parents had to tear from themselves. And the even less fortunate count the drowned 'til they can't. Only scientists could measure the journey of starlight. A thousand perfect songs you hear by yourself. A thousand belly laughs meant for someone else. A thousand lines between a thousand points of light until our ancestors stopped counting and named it all sky. A thousand butterflies that never land on you. A thousand windows rolled down to the wind, eyes always on the road. A thousand gnats, their bodies so light they blow back from your breath only to seek you again. A thousand breaths during a thousand dreams folded and folded and folded again, a thousand unfolding, creased things to let go.

Refugerequiem

Our daughter hits me, fists tiny dough balls socking my forearm. Since we are trying to teach her about consequence, I tell her I need to go sit somewhere else, without her, until she can apologize and promise to stop hitting. She is already crying, and she runs toward me, arms outstretched, and says she wants me to hold her. My resolve gives me nowhere to go but to run from her around the dining room table, and she chases me, blubbering tears, as if she were a war orphan in Vietnam and I her C-5 Galaxy. That's the way it is in this country, my mother will tell me in Vietnamese, if it were you, you'd be afraid of me spanking you. Here's the part where I make money by telling you Vietnamese people are abusive and backwards and should be glad to be living in whatever puddle or efficiency or condo or project or suburb is seen fit to contain our stink in the United States. Instead I wonder if our daughter is not as far from the war as I hoped she'd be. I wonder what ghosts made of gunpowder and spilled oil and jet stream live in her tiny muscles, if oceans drown her veins so she could run at me like this, to test the caliber of my resolve, the buoyancy of my memory, the times my body feels too small to do what I ask it to to survive, her heavy steps leaving bomb craters around the dining room table, jagged holes that will through rain and time and surviving hands become rice paddies. I pick her up and hold her; she puts her chin on my shoulder, and through teary eyes she sees everything behind me.

Acknowledgments

"Frank's Nursery and Crafts" was previously published in *Water~Stone*. "Oriental Flavor," "It Was Flame," "Cookies," "Poem for Ahmed Al-Jumaili," and "Villain/elle" were all previously published in *Asian American Literary Review*. "Lights," "When My Daughter Asks Me to Check and Make Sure Racists Can't Come In and Kill Us," and "Therapist 4" were all previously published on *diaCRITICS*. "Theresa, I Think," "Refugees from the Prom Center, the Eighties," and "Our Minnesota" were previously published in *Into Quarterly*. "Rolling through a Four-Way" was previously published in *Columbia Poetry Review,* May 2017.

Thank you to the Minnesota State Arts Board for a fellowship where this manuscript could be completed, presented, and edited.

Friends, family, community: thank you is not enough, but you have all of it that I can give.

Big thanks to my kick-ass coworkers at the Loft Literary Center, past and present, special shout-out to Jerod Santek. Thanks to the Northeast Turkey Gang writing group. Thanks to Janet Pablo and Fred Tio for generously letting me stank up their beautiful residence at Blue Water Vista, where much of this manuscript was edited to the whisper of the ocean outside the window. To the many different and wonderful communities in Minnesota who have supported me, challenged me, educated me, forgiven me: thank you. Thank you to Kundiman and all the Kundi-fam. Thank you Dr. Kelly Berg, thank you Dr. Kristina Reigstad. Thanks to photographer Anna Min for trying to make me look good—in steezy Asian men we trust. Thanks to Tyehimba Jess, Tara Betts, and Viet Thanh Nguyen—generosity beyond words. Thanks to Verna Wong and Chaun Webster of Ancestry Books, and to all the booksellers and librarians who have supported me. Thank you to everyone who ever invited me to a microphone or a gathering of ears. Thanks to everyone who has taught my work. Thank you to Coffee House Press, especially Chris Fischbach and Erika Stevens, the latter of whom made this manuscript immeasurably better. Rest in peace Allan Kornblum.

Thank you to anyone who has ever helped me, in so many ways and so much more than I could have ever hoped for.

Thanks to my family, for surviving me. I can't thank everyone I need to thank by name, or else this would be a book unto itself. But a special thank you to Juliana Hu Pegues, Sông Phi-Hu, Ed Bok Lee, R. Vincent Moniz Jr., Linda Nguyen, Kathryn Savage, Heather Wang, Shannon Gibney, Emmanuel Ortiz, Parag Khandhar, David Mura, Laurie Carlos, Diane Glancy, Diego Vazquez, Marcie Rendon, Carolyn Holbrook, Celine Liu, Scott Kurashige, Emily Lawsin, Yen Ling Shek, Mae Lee, Molly Beth Griffin, Paula Chesley, Lawrence Minh-Bui Davis, Kai Ma, Beau Sia, Dennis Kim, Su-Yoon Ko, Sajin Kwok, Siwaraya Rochanahusdin, Douglas Kearney, Giles Li, Sham-e-Ali Nayeem, Tatiana Ormaza, Adam Pine, Shá Cage, E. G. Bailey, Guante, Thuyet Nguyen, and Tony Nguyen for being keepers of this manuscript, for teaching me, for accepting my apologies, and for your support above and beyond.

LITERATURE
is not the same thing as
PUBLISHING

Coffee House Press began as a small letterpress operation in 1972 and has grown into an internationally renowned nonprofit publisher of literary fiction, essay, poetry, and other work that doesn't fit neatly into genre categories.

Coffee House is both a publisher and an arts organization. Through our *Books in Action* program and publications, we've become interdisciplinary collaborators and incubators for new work and audience experiences. Our vision for the future is one where a publisher is a catalyst and connector.

Funder Acknowledgments

Coffee House Press is an internationally renowned independent book publisher and arts nonprofit based in Minneapolis, MN; through its literary publications and *Books in Action* program, Coffee House acts as a catalyst and connector—between authors and readers, ideas and resources, creativity and community, inspiration and action.

Coffee House Press books are made possible through the generous support of grants and donations from corporations, state and federal grant programs, family foundations, and the many individuals who believe in the transformational power of literature. This activity is made possible by the voters of Minnesota through a Minnesota State Arts Board Operating Support grant, thanks to the legislative appropriation from the arts and cultural heritage fund. Coffee House also receives major operating support from the Amazon Literary Partnership, the Jerome Foundation, The McKnight Foundation, Target Foundation, and the National Endowment for the Arts (NEA). To find out more about how NEA grants impact individuals and communities, visit www.arts.gov.

Coffee House Press receives additional support from the Elmer L. & Eleanor J. Andersen Foundation; the David & Mary Anderson Family Foundation; the Buuck Family Foundation; the Dorsey & Whitney Foundation; Dorsey & Whitney LLP; the Fringe Foundation; the Knight Foundation; the Rehael Fund of the Minneapolis Foundation; the Matching Grant Program Fund of the Minneapolis Foundation; Mr. Pancks' Fund in memory of Graham Kimpton; the Schwab Charitable Fund; Schwegman, Lundberg & Woessner, P.A.; the US Bank Foundation; VSA Minnesota for the Metropolitan Regional Arts Council; and the Woessner Freeman Family Foundation in honor of Allan Kornblum.

The Publisher's Circle of Coffee House Press

Publisher's Circle members make significant contributions to Coffee House Press's annual giving campaign. Understanding that a strong financial base is necessary for the press to meet the challenges and opportunities that arise each year, this group plays a crucial part in the success of Coffee House's mission.

Recent Publisher's Circle Members include many anonymous donors, Mr. & Mrs. Rand L. Alexander, Suzanne Allen, Patricia A. Beithon, Bill Berkson & Connie Lewallen, E. Thomas Binger & Rebecca Rand Fund of the Minneapolis Foundation, Robert & Gail Buuck, Claire Casey, Louise Copeland, Jane Dalrymple-Hollo, Ruth Stricker Dayton, Jennifer Kwon Dobbs & Stefan Liess, Mary Ebert & Paul Stembler, Chris Fischbach & Katie Dublinski, Kaywin Feldman & Jim Lutz, Sally French, Jocelyn Hale & Glenn Miller, the Rehael Fund-Roger Hale/Nor Hall of the Minneapolis Foundation, Randy Hartten & Ron Lotz, Jeffrey Hom, Carl & Heidi Horsch, Amy L. Hubbard & Geoffrey J. Kehoe Fund, Kenneth Kahn & Susan Dicker, Stephen & Isabel Keating, Kenneth Koch Literary Estate, Allan & Cinda Kornblum, Leslie Larson Maheras, Sarah Lutman & Rob Rudolph, the Carol & Aaron Mack Charitable Fund of the Minneapolis Foundation, George & Olga Mack, Joshua Mack, Gillian McCain, Mary & Malcolm McDermid, Sjur Midness & Briar Andresen, Maureen Millea Smith & Daniel Smith, Peter Nelson & Jennifer Swenson, Marc Porter & James Hennessy, Enrique Olivarez, Jr. & Jennifer Komar, Robin Preble, Jeffrey Scherer, Jeffrey Sugerman & Sarah Schultz, Nan G. & Stephen C. Swid, Patricia Tilton, Stu Wilson & Melissa Barker, Warren D. Woessner & Iris C. Freeman, Margaret Wurtele, Joanne Von Blon, and Wayne P. Zink.

For more information about the Publisher's Circle and other ways to support Coffee House Press books, authors, and activities, please visit www.coffeehousepress.org/support or contact us at info@coffeehousepress.org.

This project was made possible
through generous support from

THE FRINGE FOUNDATION

Bao Phi is a multiple-time Minnesota Grand Slam poetry champ and National Poetry Slam finalist who has been on HBO's *Russell Simmons Presents Def Poetry* and whose work was included in the Best American Poetry anthology of 2006. He is the author of *Sông I Sing* and is currently the program director of the Loft Literary Center.

Thousand Star Hotel was designed by
Bookmobile Design & Digital Publisher Services.
Text is set in Arno Pro.